All-American Fighting Forces

HARLEM HELLFIGHTERS

JULIA GARSTECKI

**BLACK
RABBIT
BOOKS**

Bolt is published by Black Rabbit Books
P.O. Box 3263, Mankato, Minnesota, 56002.
www.blackrabbitbooks.com
Copyright © 2017 Black Rabbit Books

Design and Production by Michael Sellner
Photo Research by Rhonda Milbrett

Library of Congress Control Number: 2015954841

HC ISBN: 978-1-68072-002-0   PB ISBN: 978-1-68072-287-1

Printed in the United States at CG Book Printers,
North Mankato, Minnesota, 56003. 3/17

Web addresses included in this book were working and appropriate at the time of publication. The publisher is not responsible for broken or changed links.

Image Credits
Alamy: PjrStudio, 7; Art by Gary Kelley: 9, 14; deviantart.com: JesusFood, 18; Getty: MPI / Stringer, 12–13 (background); Shutterstock: Benny-Fortman, 13 (top); Gary Blakeley, 7; joshya, 19, 28–29; Markus Reed, 31; Seita, 13 (bottom); Wikimedia: Back Cover, 1, 3, 6, 10, 20–21, 26–27, 28–29 (background); American official photographer, 17; H. Charles McBarron, Jr, 4–5; Thompson, Paul, 23; Underwood &Underwood, 25, 32; Virginia Reyes of the Air Force News Agency, 7
Every effort has been made to contact copyright holders for material reproduced in this book. Any omissions will be rectified in subsequent printings if notice is given to the publisher.

Contents

CHAPTER 1

Bravery

in Battle

U.S. soldiers Johnson and Roberts hid in a **dugout**. Soon, they heard the stomp of enemy feet. Roberts ran to warn the others. Johnson threw a **grenade** at the enemies. The enemies returned fire.

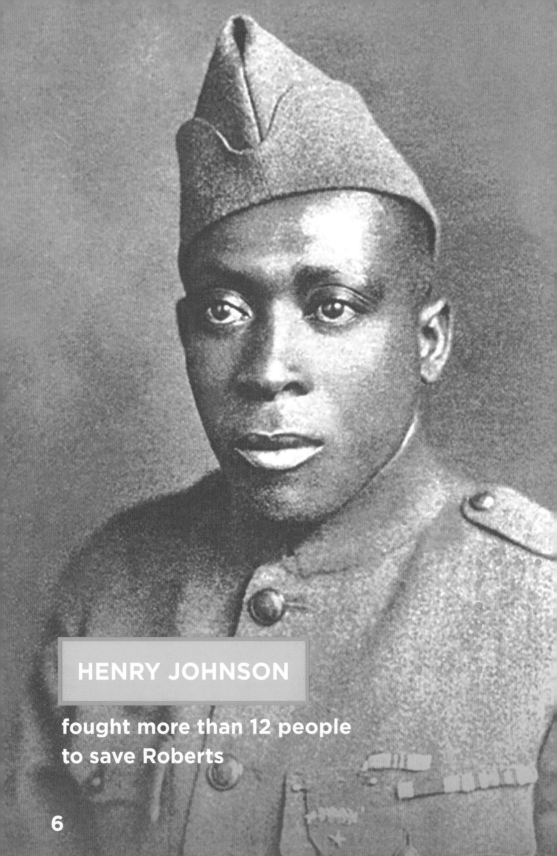

HENRY JOHNSON

fought more than 12 people to save Roberts

6

Saved

A grenade hit Roberts. He crawled back to the dugout. Johnson continued throwing grenades. Bullets hit Johnson. But he kept fighting. Suddenly, the enemy grabbed Roberts. Johnson took his knife and ran after him. He stabbed the enemies and saved Roberts.

| awarded the French War Cross in 1918 | awarded a Purple Heart in 1996 | awarded the Medal of Honor in 2015 |

The 369th

Roberts and Johnson were part of the 369th **Regiment**. This group was an African American unit. The men of this unit fought fiercely during World War I.

Many men in the 369th were from Harlem, New York. Their group became known as the "Harlem Hellfighters."

9

CHAPTER 2

New Soldiers

In the early 1900s, many whites disliked African Americans. Some whites felt blacks weren't smart or brave enough.

But then the United States joined World War I. The military needed more soldiers. The army created units for black soldiers. One of those units was the 369th.

WORLD WAR I

BY THE NUMBERS

NEARLY 1,500 HELLFIGHTERS DIED.

380,000 BLACKS IN THE U.S. MILITARY

6,000 MEN DIED EACH DAY OF THE WAR

65,038,810 total soldiers fought

369th to France

United States

Training

The 369th needed training. The men went to a military **base**. Some white people did not want black soldiers there. Groups of white people attacked the soldiers.

Many white soldiers refused to fight with black soldiers. The army sent the 369th to France.

France

CHAPTER 3

Fighting

in France

French soldiers welcomed the 369th. In France, the black soldiers learned to fight in **trenches**. They also learned to use French weapons. Then they were sent to war.

Throughout 1918, the men of the 369th fought. They helped the French fight German enemies.

Fighting in Trenches

The 369th quickly became known for its **bravery**. The men fought in trenches. In July 1918, they fought against thousands of Germans. The Germans backed away. The black soldiers chased them.

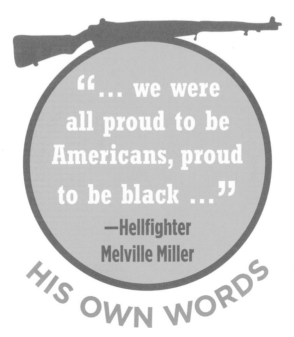

"... we were all proud to be Americans, proud to be black ..."
—Hellfighter Melville Miller

HIS OWN WORDS

LIFE IN THE TRENCHES

During World War I, soldiers lived and fought in trenches.

6 feet
(1.8 meters)
wide

· · · · · · steps
cut into the edges

7 feet
(2.1 meters)
deep

· · floor boards
to walk on

Fast Fighters

Until the war ended, the 369th fought in forests and trenches. The Hellfighters moved fast. No man of the 369th was ever taken prisoner.

Fighting ended November 11, 1918. The Harlem Hellfighters came home in February 1919.

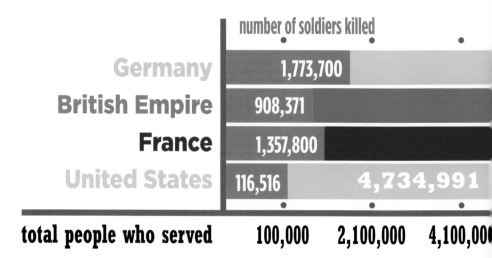

	number of soldiers killed	
Germany	1,773,700	
British Empire	908,371	
France	1,357,800	
United States	116,516	4,734,991

| total people who served | 100,000 | 2,100,000 | 4,100,000 |

11,000,000

8,904,467

8,410,000

People
Who Served
and Died in
World War I

,100,000   8,100,000   10,100,000   12,100,000

CHAPTER 4

Coming  Home

The Hellfighters spent 191 days in battle. This was longer than any other American unit. When they returned, New York City threw them a parade. Students in Harlem didn't go to school that day.

The Harlem parade was the only parade for the Hellfighters. White soldiers didn't want black soldiers in their parades.

Proved Their Strength

The men of the 369th were proud of their records. They fought long and hard. None of them were captured. And they proved African Americans were smart and brave.

APRIL 1917

The United States enters World War I.

DECEMBER 1917

The 369th arrives in France.

1917

1918

MAY 1917

Congress passes a law requiring men to register for the military.

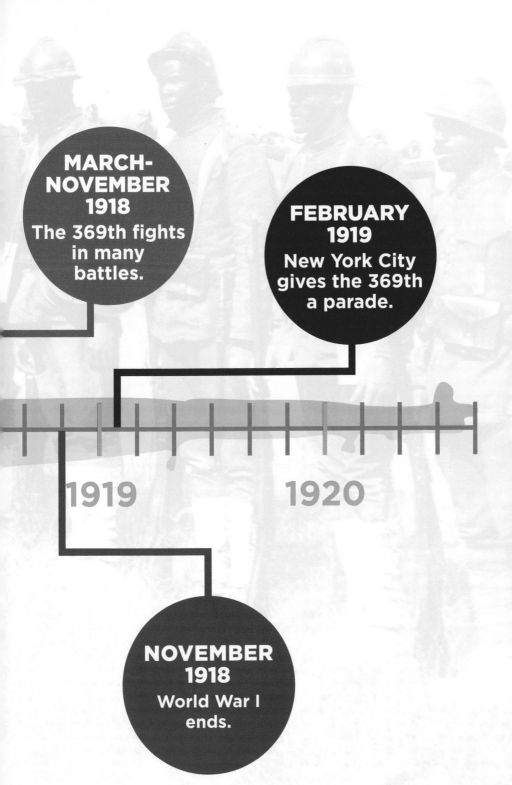

MARCH–NOVEMBER 1918
The 369th fights in many battles.

FEBRUARY 1919
New York City gives the 369th a parade.

1919

1920

NOVEMBER 1918
World War I ends.

base (BAYS)—a place where military operations begin

bravery (BRAYV-ree)—the quality that allows someone to do things that are dangerous or scary

dugout (DUG-owt)—a shelter made by digging a hole in the ground or the side of a hill

grenade (greh-NAYD)—a small bomb

regiment (REH-juh-muhnt)—a military unit made of several battalions

trench (TRENCH)—a deep, narrow hole in the ground used as protection for soldiers

BOOKS

Adams, Simon. *World War I.* Eyewitness Books. New York: DK Publishing, 2014.

Kenney, Karen Latchana. *Everything World War I.* Everything Series. Washington, D.C.: National Geographic Society, 2014.

Lewis, J. Patrick. *Harlem Hellfighters.* Mankato, MN: Creative Editions, 2014.

WEBSITES

The Harlem Hellfighters
www.youtube.com/watch?v=eEuoAl1elLU

Interactive WWI Timeline
theworldwar.org/explore/interactive-wwi-timeline

Life at Home During the First World War
www.ngkids.co.uk/history/life-at-home-during-WWI

World War I for Kids: Trench Warfare
www.ducksters.com/history/world_war_i/trench_warfare.php

INDEX